# The Lorna Doone Trail

S. H. Burton

## The Exmoor Press

This Selection from *Lorna Doone,* the Introduction and the
Commentary © S. H. Burton, 1975

The Photographs © The Exmoor Press, 1975

Second impression 1985
Third impression 1992
Fourth impression 1998

ISBN 0 900131 19 5

British Library Cataloguing-in-Publication-Data
CIP data for this book is available from the British Library

MICROSTUDIES
Each Microstudy has been written by an expert and is designed to
appeal to all who are interested in Exmoor

A list of the titles in the Microstudy Series is available from
The Exmoor Press    Dulverton    Somerset

Trade Distribution by
HALSGROVE
Halsgrove House
Lower Moor Way
Tiverton
Devon, EX16 6SS
01884 243242
01884 243325
http://www.halsgrove.com

*Front Cover:* Jan Ridd and Ruth Huckaback, by Rowland Wheelwright
(from the 1925 Harrap edition of *Lorna Doone)*
*Back Cover:* Oare Church (courtesy of Exmoor National Park)

Williton Printers, Somerset

# Contents

★

## Illustrations

Inside Back Cover Map of Doone Land by Robert Winn

The author took the photographs facing pages 26, 28, 30, 32 and 34. All the other photographs are by
Mike Naylor

The photographic processing was carried out by Andrew Priddy, of Minehead.

3

# The Author

Author of over fifty books—ranging from Shakespearian criticism to ghost stories and from science fiction to linguistic texts—his regional writing has always played a leading part in S. H. Burton's career. Among his many books in that field are *The West Country, Devon Villages* and *A West Country Anthology*—all published by Robert Hale.

His *Exmoor* (Fourth Edition, Robert Hale, 1984) was first published by Hodder and Stoughton in 1969 and was chosen by *Books and Bookmen* as its 'Country Book of the Year'.

S. H. Burton's books are admired for their 'rare skill' *(The Field)* and 'sheer delight' *(The Sunday Times)*. Readers of *The Lorna Doone Trail* will find those same qualities in this detailed study of R. D. Blackmore's fictional use of the Doone legends.

★

This book is for Felicity Hodder-Williams
whose idea it was

# Introduction

## R. D. Blackmore

'The last Victorian'—so one of his biographers (Kenneth Budd) called him. Another (W. H. Dunn) characterised him as:

> . . . the very incarnation of England . . . John Bull, with all John's virtues, idiosyncrasies, stubbornness, kindliness, touchiness, aloofness, provincialism, patriotism . . .

There is truth in both descriptions, but Blackmore's own assertion is more relevant to the purposes of this book:

> In everything, except the accident of birth, I am Devonian; my ancestry were all Devonians; my sympathies and feeling are all Devonian . . .

The explorer of the *Lorna Doone* trail will come closest to Blackmore and to an appreciation of his best-known book by seeing him in his own beloved West Country setting.

Nor will such an explorer forget what Blackmore himself was always careful to stress: Devonian though the author felt himself to be, his hero, Jan Ridd, was a yeoman and churchwarden 'of the parish of Oare, in the County of Somerset'. Blackmore's own most formative years were spent in the company of relatives to whom West Somerset was as familiar as North Devon. The modern traveller who follows Jan's adventures must cross and recross the meandering county boundary. 'Lorna Doone Country' is quintessential Exmoor—part in Somerset, part in Devon; and, since all the most stirring deeds described in the book take place on the moor, Blackmore could not draw—and had no wish to draw—an artificial division between the two counties.

'The accident of birth' made Blackmore a native of Longworth in North Berkshire, where his father, the Rev. John Blackmore, was Curate-in-Charge. The accident of death, together with John Blackmore's longing to return to more congenial scenes, brought the infant boy to Culmstock in East Devon. In the autumn of 1825, just three months after Blackmore's birth, an outbreak of typhus fever ravaged Longworth. Among those who died were Blackmore's mother, her twin sister, and most of the family servants.

A year later, John Blackmore accepted a curacy at Culmstock, there marrying, in 1831, his second wife—Blackmore's loved and loving stepmother—and quitting that pretty village in 1835 for Ashford, not far from Barnstaple. (Many years later, in 1894, Culmstock became the 'Perlycross' in Blackmore's novel of that name.)

The move to Ashford was indeed a homecoming. The Blackmore family traced its line back to the late 16th century when 'Richard Blackmore and Jane his wiefe' were renting land in Parracombe. John Blackmore, the novelist's grandfather, was rector of Combe Martin and Oare. Richard, his uncle, was rector of Charles. The Exmoor landscape was 'plotted and pieced' with Blackmore names and associations. The power of this landscape and of the family associations over an imaginative boy's mind is revealed in Blackmore's vivid reminiscence of his childhood:

> I behold an old man, with a keen profile, under a parson's shovel hat, riding a tall chestnut horse up the western slope of Exmoor, followed by his little grandson upon a shaggy and stuggy pony.

It was a family tradition, too, that took R. D. Blackmore to the West Country's most famous school. He entered Blundell's in 1837, leaving it for Exeter College, Oxford, in 1843. Later in this book the impact of his schooldays is discussed, for Blackmore, Blundell's and *Lorna Doone* are inseparable. Here, in this very brief account of his life, we can follow the course of his happy and hard-working days at Oxford. There, he was recognized as a good classical scholar and known for his quiet ways and fierce independence of mind. A contemporary remembered him as a good angler, a skilful chess player, a keen naturalist—and a good friend.

After Oxford he turned to the law and was called to the Bar in 1855. Three years later he abandoned his legal career in consequence of the epileptic attacks that now, and for some years to come, plagued him. An outdoor life was considered essential and, after filling in some years as a schoolmaster, he bought a 16-acre plot of land at Teddington on which he built Gomer House. Then a village, 21 miles from the centre of London, Teddington offered Blackmore that rural environment for which he craved. As W. H. Dunn pointed out, some sentences from *Clara Vaughan* (1864) accurately describe his own tastes and needs:

> Vigorous and elastic as I am, I cannot deny that the air and weather have great dominion over me. It was always so with my dear father. Two days spent indoors, without any real exercise, would make him feel as uneasy as a plant in a cellaret . . . when he had lost his fishing or shooting or bit of gardening too long, he was unlike himself . . . I too am not of a sedentary nature, though upon due occasion I can sit writing or drawing for some hours together. But how fine a thing all the while to see any motion outside—a leaf that can skip, or a cloud that can run! How we envy a sparrow his little hop, even across the gutter.

Teddington's proximity to the London markets was another reason for Blackmore's choice of this as his permanent home. He specialised in vegetable and fruit growing, tackling his new work with a care for detail, a patience, a determination, and an intelligence that speedily won for him renown as a horticulturalist. Unfortunately, renown butters no parsnips and, in forty years of hard and skilful work, Blackmore 'only twice made ends meet'. He attributed his lack of financial success primarily to the competition of cheap fruit imported from California.

Earlier in life Blackmore had experimented with poetry. Now, in a long battle with adversity, he turned to novel writing as a means of supplementing his income—'I must ply the pen to pay for the spade,' he wrote to a friend. His industry was prodigious. Between 1854 and 1897 he published fourteen novels, seven volumes of verse and one volume of short stories—all this in addition to full-time labour in his market garden. In his most prolific period he averaged one long work of fiction—none of his novels is short!—every two-and-a-half years.

Today, while everybody knows of *Lorna Doone*, his other books are forgotten. Even in his lifetime, he suffered neglect from the public while enjoying the praise of some eminent critics. The truth was that he was born too late. His novels—bulky and, despite a great narrative gift in individual scenes, slow-moving—were out of fashion. The day of the three-volume novel was done—and Blackmore knew it. 'I have finished my last novel,' he said when *Dariel* came out in 1897, 'and it is high time to stop'. He was then 72 years old, tired and ill. His wife had died in 1888 after many years of indifferent health, and Blackmore felt his childless loneliness keenly. His humour and independence sustained him to the end. Who can fail to admire and love the man who, though tormented by rheumatism, could write to a friend like this?

> Sad is my fate, and sad my phiz.
> I am devoured with rheumatiz;
> And the more I am rubbed, the worse it is.

In similar vein, he described his doctors' attempts to alleviate his condition:

> What thumping fees they charged. Oh laws!
> For 'best advice procurable'.
> But now my hopes revive, because
> I am pronounced incurable.

He died on 20 January 1900; four years later, a memorial window and a marble portrait were dedicated to his memory in Exeter Cathedral. Words spoken at the ceremony by another famous West Country writer, Eden Phillpotts, are the fittest of epitaphs for Richard Doddridge Blackmore:

> He indicated the virtue of courage and humility, the propriety of tolerance, the value of self-reliance, the distinction of patience . . . His splendid generosity, his genius for finding out the worth in others, his charity and his humour, made Blackmore a man apart . . . There was in his broad sweep, like the roll of an ocean wave, something Elizabethan . . . Absolutely fearless, he answered only to his own ideals, and not the most arrogant critic of literature dared to handle his work as severely as he did himself.

## Lorna Doone

The enduring popularity of *Lorna Doone*—in films, on television, and in book form—may easily blind us to the fact that it sold slowly at first. Blackmore described its delayed success in his characteristically ironical way:

> . . . *Lorna Doone* narrowly shaved the brink of Lethe. Indeed . . . of the first 500 copies, only about 300 were sold . . . It is the merest fluke that *Lorna Doone* was ever heard of any more . . . whether from the advent of the Marquis of Lorne, or some fashionable freak, the book began to run, when on its last legs.

'The advent of the Marquis of Lorne' was one of those strokes of luck that sometimes—all-too-rarely—bring a totally unexpected windfall to an author. In 1870 Princess Louise, daughter of Queen Victoria, was betrothed to the Marquis of Lorne. Blackmore often told how a reviewer of *Lorna Doone* quite mistakenly said that the book was written about the ancestors of the Marquis—'and then everybody read it, out of curiosity, and exhausted nearly a score of editions'.

We know now, however, that this happy mistake was by no means the real reason for the book's success. Once attention had been directed to the novel it was found to contain the essential ingredients of a best-seller; faithful love between a high-born, beautiful girl and her heroic, single-minded lover; the triumph of youth, beauty and truth over hatred, lies, oppression and cruelty; a superb villain; a wild and brilliantly delineated background; exciting deeds; suspense; humour; a strong cast of supporting characters—*Lorna Doone* has everything.

Whether the Doones ever existed or not is a complex issue, deserving (and frequently receiving) a book to itself. Here, it is sufficient to say that Blackmore did not invent the Doone legends on which he based his book. From childhood he had been familiar with the many moorland versions of the Doone stories; familiar, too, with the various printed references to those vicious outlaws, one source of which (Thomas Henry Cooper's *Guide to Lynton*) pre-dated *Lorna Doone* by sixteen years. His own unquestioning acceptance of the Doones gave utter conviction to his writing about them. While the book was in progress he revisited Devon and Somerset. Porlock, Charles Rectory, Oare and Withypool—a signed letter from Blackmore hangs in the bar of the Royal Oak there to this very day—were among the places in which he refreshed his memory, tirelessly interviewing Exmoor folk and 'putting it all down in a notebook'.

But the vividness of the style and the exuberance of the storytelling are proof enough that *Lorna Doone* came from the heart. If ever a book welled out of the dearest of a man's affections it is this. Those Exmoor days of long ago come to life in these pages: scenes, setting and story were a labour of love. As Blackmore said some years after its publication:

> Nothing has pleased me more than the great success of this simple tale. For truly it is a grand success to win the attention and kind regard, not of the general public only, but also of those who are at home with the scenery, people, life and language, wherein a native cannot always satisfy the natives.

And the general public as well as the natives have gladly continued to yield their 'attention and kind regard' to this best-loved of all romances.

### The Lorna Doone Story

In his preface to the first edition Blackmore himself shrewdly indicated the sources of the book's power:

> . . . any son of Exmoor, chancing on this volume, cannot fail to bring to mind the nurse-tales of his childhood—the savage deeds of the Doones . . . the beauty of the hapless maid brought up in the midst of them, the plain John Ridd's Herculean power, and . . . the exploits of Tom Faggus.

Set in the reigns of Charles II and James II, the novel has as its historical background Monmouth's tragic rebellion. Judge Jeffreys' fearsome personality plays a part in the story, and both John Ridd and Tom Faggus, the highwayman, were—in Exmoor lore—more than mere fictions.

Called home from Blundell's School by the news of his father's murder at the hands of the Doones, John—or Jan—Ridd devotes himself to the welfare of his mother and his sisters at Plover's Barrows Farm. A chance meeting with Lorna when he is fourteen and has made the perilous ascent into the Doone Valley colours his mind with memories of her, and puts him in possession of the secret entrance to the outlaws' fastness. When Jan is twenty-one he enters Glen Doone again, the first of a series of stolen and dangerous meetings in which he wins Lorna's heart.

The death of Sir Ensor Doone leaves Lorna unprotected, and during a great snow Jan carries her off to Plover's Barrows to save her from a forced marriage to Carver Doone. The wiles of Counsellor Doone and the savagery of Carver threaten the happiness of Jan and Lorna, but eventually it is discovered that Lorna is a direct descendant not of Sir Ensor Doone but of Scottish ancestors named Dugal. On her mother's side, she is descended from the Lords of Lorne—themselves connected by marriage with the Doones. Now, her high birth and wealth interpose a barrier between Lady Lorna Dugal and the yeoman John Ridd. However, her fidelity and Jan's great services to her kinsman and Guardian in Chancery, Earl Brandir of Lochawe, ensure for the Somerset farmer signal marks of royal favour. James II knights Jan and pardons him for his innocent involvement in the Monmouth rebellion. At Judge Jeffreys' instigation—and greatly to his profit—the rich heiress is freed from her Chancery wardship and receives royal approval for her marriage to Sir John Ridd.

Infuriated by another Doone outrage, the Exmoor people, led by Jan, finally storm the Doone Valley, only Carver escaping their just vengeance. Shortly afterwards, Jan and Lorna are married in Oare Church, but Carver shoots Lorna at the altar. Believing her dead, Jan rides after the villain and brings him to bay at the Wizard's Slough. After a mighty struggle, Jan triumphs and the defeated and maddened Carver is engulfed by the fearful bog. Both Jan and Lorna recover from their wounds and live happily ever after.

9

## The Lorna Doone Trail

Through words and pictures this book traces the Exmoor adventures of Jan and Lorna and of some of the most important secondary characters, such as Jeremy Stickles and Tom Faggus. Beginning with Jan's sad journey home from school, it follows the hero and heroine to their ideally happy ending. Blackmore's own words are, of course, of prime authority—and are so employed; but I have added my own commentaries, knowing how often the complexities of the plot and Blackmore's heightened treatment of scene and place baffle the explorer. It is only fair to remind ourselves that he was writing a novel, not a guide-book: was, in his own words, 'shaping this old tale' in which 'the incidents, characters, time and scenery are alike romantic'.

Mere 'identification', then, has never been my main purpose since, where much must remain conjectural, dogmatic assertion would have been foolish and misleading. Where positive statements could be made I have not avoided them, for lovers of the novel will receive added pleasure from following confidently in Blackmore's footsteps.

Above all, I have tried, in this small compass, so to choose quotations and illustrations as to capture something of the novel's abounding life—thus hoping to draw my readers back to *Lorna Doone* itself.

# The Lorna Doone Trail

$M$Y father . . . being a great admirer of learning, and well able to write his name, sent me, his only son, to be schooled at Tiverton. For the chief boast of that ancient town (next to its woollen-staple) is a worthy grammar-school, the largest in the west of England, founded and handsomely endowed in the year 1604, by Master Peter Blundell, of that same place, clothier . . .

The school-house stands beside a stream . . . called 'Lowman' which . . . is wont to flood into a mighty head of waters . . . and most of all when its little co-mate, called the 'Taunton brook' . . . comes foaming down like a great roan horse . . . Then are the grey stone walls of Blundell on every side encompassed . . . And in the very front of the gate, just without the archway, where the ground is paved most handsomely, you may see in copy-letters done a great P.B. of white pebbles. Now, it is the custom and the law that when the waxing element lips though it be but a single pebble of the founder's letters, it is in the licence of any boy, soever small and un-doctrined, to rush into the great school-rooms . . . and scream at the top of his voice, 'P.B.'

Then, with a yell, the boys leap up . . . toss their caps to the black-beamed roof, and haply the very books after them . . . Then the masters look at one another . . . and with a spirited bang they close their books, and make invitation the one to the other for pipes and foreign cordials, recommending the chance of the time, and the comfort away from cold water.

CHAPTER I

*According to the novel, John Ridd left Blundell's on 29 November 1673, but Blackmore depicts the school and its customs very much as they were in his own schooldays (1837-1843). Little, probably, had changed between 1604 and the earlier years of the 19th century, and Blackmore was very much a product of the old school. Indeed, the 'P.B.' tradition was kept up until the late 1950s—and this despite the fact that the P.B. stones had been moved from Old Blundell's and placed outside the gates of the 'new' school which was built (in 1880-1882) on a spacious site about a mile to the east of the original founda-tion. One of the finest examples of Jacobean 'domestic' architecture in the West Country, Old Blundell's now belongs to the National Trust. Peter Blundell planned on a munificent scale. The Lord Chief Justice of England was his executor and the school was, as Blackmore puts it, a 'chief boast' of Tiverton—then, and for many a year after-wards, a prosperous centre of the wool trade.*

**Old Blundell's, Tiverton**

W̲ᴇ left the town of the two fords, which they say is the meaning of it, very early in the morning, after lying one day to rest, as was demanded by the nags, sore of foot and foundered. For my part, too, I was glad to rest, having aches all over me, and very heavy bruises; and we lodged at the sign of the White Horse Inn, in the street called Gold Street, opposite where the souls are of John and Joan Greenway, set up in gold letters, because we must take the homeward way at cockcrow of the morning.

CHAPTER III

*Small wonder that John ached all over after his epic fight with Robin Snell (see Chapter II). Fought out on the famous 'Ironing Box'—'as the triangle of turf is called, where the two causeways coming from the school-porch and the hall-porch meet'—this struggle resulted in victory for the Exmoor boy, whose heart had responded to John Fry's call: 'Never thee knack under, Jan, or never coom naigh Hexmoor no more'.*

*At this stage of the story, Jan does not know that his father has been murdered. John Fry keeps the truth from him and he wonders whether 'father had sent for me, because he had a good harvest, and the rats were bad in the corn-chamber'.*

*The White Horse Inn still stands, its front much altered, but its great entrance yet demonstrating how important it was to travellers in coaching and pack-horse days. Opposite, the Greenway Almshouses (1529) testify to the pious benevolence of John and Joan Greenway— benefactors also of St. Peter's Church, Tiverton's chief architectural glory. Both in the church and on the walls of his almshouses, John Greenway inscribed prayers for his soul and conjured the passer-by to pray with him: 'Pray for the souls of John and Jone'; 'God speed our waye. Pray for the soul of John Grenwaye'; 'Have grace, ye men, and ever pray For the soul of John and Jone Grenwaye'. As Martin Dunsford ('History of Tiverton', 1790) wrote: 'By some of his inscriptions . . . he seems to have been strongly impressed with dread of a future state of Purgatory'.*

*Wool and religion, fire and flood, the siege of the Castle, the uproar of reform, industrial decline, the Heathcoat renaissance, and now 'key settlement and development status'—such is the history of this bustling, friendly West Country town: 'town of the two fords', nurse of John Ridd's youthful years, birthplace of so many famous men.*

**Greenway's Almshouses, Tiverton**

Fʀᴏᴍ Tiverton town to the town of Oare is a very long and painful road, and in good truth the traveller must make his way, as the saying is; for the way is still unmade, at least, on this side of Dulverton, although there is less danger now than in the time of my schooling; for now a good horse may go there without much cost of leaping; but when I was a boy, the spurs would fail, when needed most, by reason of the slough-cake. It is to the credit of this age, and our advance upon fatherly ways, that now we have laid down rods and fagots, and even stump-oaks here and there, so that a man in good daylight need not sink, if he be quite sober. There is nothing I have striven at more than doing my duty, way-warden over Exmoor.

CHAPTER III

*In his assumed character of John Ridd, Blackmore refers to 'the town of Oare'; but Oare is, and has always been, a hamlet. 'Township' means settlement or inhabited place. The rest of the description is strictly accurate. Until the development of turnpikes in the late eighteenth century and the Knight family's purchase of the Forest in the early 19th century, there were no roads on Exmoor. Wheeled vehicles were rare: sledges ('trackamucks') were in common use. The road from Tiverton to Bampton did not follow the Exe Valley. Until fairly recent times roads always climbed high, out of the wet lands and the woods. John Ridd and the faithful, though often cowardly, John Fry would leave Tiverton by Bampton Street and Higher Bampton Street. Then, up over Red Hill and Knightshayes— no mansion there in those days—and through the wandering hilly lanes to Bampton. They did not pause in that pleasant little town, for their first 'baiting-place' was to be Dulverton.*

*They would leave Bampton by the road shown in this illustration, taking the high route out of the 'pony fair town' (the Fair has always been, and still is, held on the last Thursday in October), quitting the wide main street and the stylish architecture as they climbed up what is now called the 'B 3222'. This led them, as it leads us, to High Cross—where the ghostly chains rattle on winter nights— and past Combe Head until, at the summit of Grant's Hill, they would see their first Exmoor panorama. Then, a long drop down towards Higher Grant's Farm—nearly out of Devon, but so typically Devonian in its beauty—swinging left at the old toll house (not there in John Ridd's day) and into charming Exebridge, where Devon ends and Somerset begins.*

**Bampton: the Dulverton road**

16

THE road from Bampton to Dulverton had not been very delicate, yet nothing to complain of much—no deeper, indeed, than the hocks of a horse, except in the rotten places.

CHAPTER III

For the day-boys [of Blundell's] had brought us word that some [packmen] intending their way to the town [of Tiverton] ... must be in ere nightfall, because Mr. Faggus was after them. Now Mr. Faggus was my first cousin, and an honour to the family, being a North Molton man, of great renown on the highway, from Barum town even to London.

CHAPTER II

Much cause he had to be harsh with the world; and yet all acknowledged him pleasant, when a man gave up his money ... By trade he had been a blacksmith, in the town of North Molton ... a rough rude place at the end of Exmoor; so that many people marvelled if such a man was bred there. Not only could he read and write, but he had solid substance; a piece of land worth a hundred pounds, and right of common for two hundred sheep, and a score-and-a-half of beasts ... and made such a fame at the shoeing of horses, that the farriers of Barum were like to lose their custom ... when suddenly, like a thunderbolt, a lawyer's writ fell upon him ... This was the beginning of a law-suit with Sir Robert Bampfylde, a gentleman of the neighbourhood, who tried to oust him from his common, and drove his cattle, and harassed them. And by that suit of law poor Tom was ruined altogether ... and he took it to heart so grievously that he said, 'The world hath preyed on me, like a wolf. God help me now to prey on the world'. ... Everybody cursed the Doones, who lived apart disdainfully. But all good people liked Mr. Faggus—when he had not robbed them—and many a poor sick man or woman blessed him for other people's money; and all the hostlers, stable-boys and tapsters entirely worshipped him.

CHAPTER XII

*The road to Dulverton would have been a greater ordeal but for this fine old bridge over the Exe. Here, just below the confluence of the Barle and the Exe rivers, is the vital crossing place—and here has stood for centuries an inn for the refreshment of man and beast.*

*Tom Faggus—a West Country Robin Hood—plays a large part in the story. He marries Jan Ridd's sister Annie and is involved in both the Doone plot and the Monmouth rebellion. Finally, he reforms. Blackmore did not invent Faggus. According to legend, he was captured in the inn at Exebridge. His famous strawberry mare, Winnie, was shot, and the intrepid highwayman was hanged at Taunton.*

**The Bridge and the Anchor, Exebridge**

IT was high noon before we were got to Dulverton that day . . . My mother had an uncle living there, but we were not to visit his house this time, at which I was somewhat astonished, since we needs must stop for at least two hours, to bait our horses thorough well, before coming to the black bogway . . . But now, at Dulverton, we dined upon the rarest and choicest victuals that ever I did taste. Even now, at my time of life, to think of it gives me appetite, as once and awhile to think of my first love makes me love all goodness. Hot mutton pasty was a thing I had often heard of from wealthy boys and men, who made a dessert of dinner; and to hear them talk of it made my lips smack, and my ribs come inwards.

And now John Fry strode into the hostel, with the air and grace of a short-legged man, and shouted as loud as if he was calling sheep upon Exmoor: 'Hot mootton pasty for two trarv'lers, at number vaive, in vaive minnits! Dish un up in the tin with the grahvy, zame as I hardered last Tuesday'.

Of course it did not come in five minutes, nor yet in ten . . . but that made it all the better when it came . . . and the smell of it was enough to make an empty man thank God for the room there was inside him. Fifty years have passed me quicker than the taste of that gravy.

CHAPTER III

*Still unaware that his father is dead, John Ridd smacks his lips over his Dulverton food—as many a traveller has done since his day. We cannot be certain which Dulverton hostelry Blackmore had in mind: within living memory there were a score of taverns and hotels in the delectable little town. Today, the Lamb, the Lion, the Bridge and the Rock are the sole but proud survivors of a goodly company.*

*It is at the inn that the boy first encounters the mysterious foreign lady's-maid whose fate is bound up with the Doones. Later, he sees her again, travelling, with her mistress and two children, to Watchet on a journey destined to end tragically.*

*Throughout the novel Blackmore depicts Dulverton as a moorland metropolis, where luxuries may be purchased and where news of the great world abounds. This illustration emphasises the importance of its site. Sheltered in its deep bowl, it drew ample water power from the Barle for its fulling and grist mills. Busy shops—then as now— served the scattered moorland folk; and it was at Dulverton that the roads ended and 'the black bogway' began.*

**Dulverton—from the north**

20

M R. REUBEN HUCKABACK, whom many good folk in Dulverton will remember long after my time, was my mother's uncle . . . He owned the very best shop in the town, and did a fine trade in soft ware, especially when the pack-horses came safely in at Christmas-time . . . And truly, the Dulverton people said that he was the richest man in their town, and could buy up half the county armigers; ay, and if it came to that, they would like to see any man, at Bampton, or at Wiveliscombe, and you might say almost Taunton, who could put down golden Jacobus and Carolus against him . . . Now it pleased God . . . (in spite of all the fogs) to send safe home to Dulverton, and what was more, with their loads quite safe, a goodly string of pack-horses. Nearly half of their charge was for Uncle Reuben, and he knew how to make the most of it. Then, having balanced his debits and credits, and set writs running against defaulters, as behoves a good Christian at Christmas-tide, he saddled his horse, and rode off towards Oare . . .

**CHAPTER XIII**

*Jan's Uncle Reuben is a comic character who plays an indirect but important part in the story. Grandfather of Ruth—who loves Jan and saves his life when the doctors are bleeding him to death— he opens a mine near the Wizard's Slough and is thus instrumental in reuniting the mine 'Captain', Simon Carfax, with his daughter, Gwenny, who is Lorna's maid and companion. Reuben Huckaback is also an ingenious conspirator when the downfall of the Doones is being planned. His position as the wealthiest man in Dulverton reinforces Blackmore's insistence on the importance and prosperity of the town.*

*This photograph of a typical corner of old Dulverton brings out the enduring character of the place. Along cobbled alleys such as this, Reuben Huckaback would have walked to worship in church—or to dun his debtors! The essence of the town lies in its narrow streets and shy courts, hidden from the careless passer-by. Since its personality is threatened by ever-increasing traffic and has been damaged by the short-sighted decisions of planners, readers of this book may well treasure a glimpse of Dulverton that R. D. Blackmore—or, indeed, Jan Ridd—would have recognized.*

*Beyond this lane lies the hilly road that John Ridd and John Fry took together—the hill up which 'the Oare folk and the Watchet folk must trudge on together' until their ways parted.*

**Church Lane, Dulverton**

MERCY of God! Where be us now?' said John Fry, waking suddenly; 'us ought to have passed hold hash, Jan. Zeen it on the road, have 'ee?'

'No indeed, John; no old ash. Nor nothing else to my knowing; nor heard nothing, save thee snoring'.

'Watt a vule thee must be then, Jan; and me myzell no better. Harken, lad, harken!'

We drew our horses up and listened, through the thickness of the air, and with our hands laid to our ears . . . Then there came a mellow noise, very low and mournsome, not a sound to be afraid of, but to long to know the meaning, with a soft rise of the hair. Three times it came and went again . . . and then I touched John Fry to know that there was something near me.

'Doon't 'e be a vule, Jan! Vaine moozick as iver I 'eer. God bless the man as made un doo it.'

'Have they hanged one of the Doones then, John?'

'Hush, lad; never talk laike o' thiccy. Hang a Doone! God knoweth the King would hang pretty quick, if her did.'

'Then who is it in chains, John?' . . .

'It be nawbody,' said John, 'vor us to make a fush about. Belong to t'other zide o' the moor, and come staling shape to our zide. Red Jem Hannaford his name. Thank God for him to be hanged, lad; and good cess to his soul for craiken' zo.'

So the sound of the quiet swinging led us . . . even as far as the foot of the gibbet where the four cross-ways are.

'Vamous job this here,' cried John . . . 'Red Jem, too, and no doubt of him; he do hang so handsome like, and his ribs up laike a horse a'most. God bless them as discoovered the way to make a rogue so useful. Good naight to thee, Jem, my lad; and not break thy drames with the craiken'.'

. . . I was sorry for Red Jem . . . But John would talk no more about it . . . 'Hould thee tongue, lad,' he said sharply; 'us be naigh the Doone-track now, two maile from Dunkery Beacon . . . So happen they be abroad tonight, us must crawl on our belly-places, boy.'

CHAPTER III

*Although Chibbet (Gibbet) Post is more than two miles from Dunkery Beacon, that is almost certainly the place where Red Jem was hanging and providing such a useful landmark for benighted travellers. Jan Ridd and John Fry are well clear of Dulverton now and heading for Plover's Barrows. Even as the crow flies, they still have about seven moorland miles—and the perils of the Doones—ahead.*

**Chibbet Post—near Exford**

OFTENTIMES I looked at his gun, an ancient piece found in the sea . . . and it hurt me to see how John handled it, as if he had no memory. 'Bad job for he, as her had not got thiccy, the naight as her coom acrass them Doones . . . a maight have been gooin' to market now, 'stead of laying banked up, over yanner. Maister Jan, thee can zee the grave if thee look alang this here goonbarryel . . .'

CHAPTER VI

Almost everybody knows . . . how pleasant and soft the fall of the land is round about Plover's Barrows Farm. All above it is strong dark mountain, spread with heath, and desolate, but near our house the valleys cove, and open warmth and shelter . . . And indeed a stout good piece of it [the brook] comes through our farm yard and swells sometimes to a rush of waves when the clouds are on the hill-tops . . . But about two miles below our farm, the Badgworthy water runs into the Lynn and makes a real river of it.

CHAPTER VII

*The popularity of 'Lorna Doone' has stimulated numerous pamphlets that have sought to prove that Plover's Barrows Farm was* here *or that the Doone Valley was* there. *It is a waste of time to attempt this kind of identification. Blackmore knew that his novel was a romance and he would have laughed himself silly at the efforts of self-styled 'researchers' to pin him down. The topographical 'interpretations' of 'Lorna Doone' cancel each other out if the reader brings a grain of commonsense—and the evidence of the Ordnance Survey Map—to bear on the blinkered interpretations of fanatics who have stridently argued their so-called cases.*

*'Farmer Snow came* up *to Plover's Barrows'. Well, he could have done so just as plausibly if he had lived at the present Lorna Doone Farm and the Ridds had lived at Oare Ford Farm or if their respective conjectural domiciles had been inter-changed. I instance this merely as one example of the kind of useless 'trump-card' that the protagonists use in their arguments.*

*We can get no sense out of these sterile debates. Better, simply, to enjoy the book—recognize that Blackmore based the novel on his memories of 'Doone Country'. Unless we are sensible we shall litter the Exmoor landscape with as many debatable 'Plover's Barrows Farms' and 'Water Slides' as there were fragments of 'the true cross' in medieval Europe.*

*The illustration shows an Exmoor farmhouse nearer in every detail to what Blackmore had in his imaginative mind than any other site.*

**Lorna Doone Farm, Malmsmead**

26

THENCE it hurries away, with strength and a force of wilful waters, under the foot of a bare-faced hill, and so to rocks and woods again, where the stream is covered over, and dark, heavy pools delay it. There are plenty of fish all down this way, and the further you go the bigger they be, having deeper grounds to feed in . . . yet it so happened that neither my sister Annie . . . nor I had been up the Badgworthy Water . . . For Badgworthy Water ran out of Doone Valley, a mile or so from the mouth of it.

. . . suddenly, in an open space, where meadows spread about it, I found a good stream flowing softly into the body of our brook. And it brought, so far as I could guess by the sweep of it under my knee-caps, a larger power of clear water than the Lyn itself had; only it came more quietly down, not being troubled with stairs and steps as the fortune of the Lyn is, but gliding smoothly and forcibly, as if upon some set purpose. Hereupon I drew up, and thought . . . it was a frightful thing . . . to venture, where no grown man durst, up the Badgworthy Water . . . However . . . my spirit rose within me . . . and crossing the Lyn I went stoutly up under the branches which hang so dark on the Badgworthy river.

CHAPTER VII

*The romantic aspects of Blackmore's descriptions of 'Doone Land' scenery are illustrated by those extracts. The first paragraph purports to be a description of the East Lyn, but is couched in such general terms that it could apply to any one of a dozen Exmoor rivers in their lower courses. Then comes the ominous mention of Badgworthy Water which neither Annie nor Jan has explored, because 'Badgworthy Water ran out of Doone Valley'. That statement alone should have put paid to the amateur detective work of the 'Doone Valley sleuths'. Nothing on the ground supports Blackmore's imagined relationship between Badgworthy and the various tributary combes that feed it.*

*The illustration shows the junction between Hoccombe Water and Long Combe where, under the molinia-clad ridge of Trout Hill, these two moorland valleys meet and turn due north to form Badgworthy. From this confluence—rarely seen by those who enter Badgworthy from the Malmsmead end—the lovely stream deepens until it adds its waters to the East Lyn. Badgworthy does not run out of anything: several small tributaries enter it before it joins Oare Water and then becomes the East Lyn. Blackmore's description gives a heightened idea of Badgworthy's power; though its beauty cannot be exaggerated. Again—see the Introduction—one should remember that he was writing a novel, not a guide-book.*

**Badgworthy begins where Hoccombe Water
and Long Combe meet**

FOR she stood at the head of a deep green valley, carved from out the mountains in a perfect oval, with a fence of sheer rock standing round it, eighty feet or a hundred high; from whose brink black wooded hills swept up to the sky-line. By her side a little river glided out . . . lapsed away, and fell into the valley . . . further down, on either bank, were covered houses, built of stone, square and roughly cornered, set as if the brook were meant to be the street between them. Only one room high they were, and not placed opposite each other, but in and out as skittles are; only that the first of all, which proved to be the captain's, was a sort of double house, or rather two houses joined together by a plank-bridge over the river.

Fourteen cots my mother counted, all very much of a pattern . . . Deep in the quiet valley there, away from noise, and violence, and brawl, save that of the rivulet, any man would have deemed them homes of simple mind and innocence. Yet not a single house stood there but was the home of murder.

CHAPTER IV

*The above description of the outlaws' stronghold tallies with those given later in the book, though the Water Slide and Doone Gate are added as dramatic features in further episodes.*

*The most important words in Blackmore's first account of the dreaded valley make the ironical statement that 'any man would have deemed them [the Doone houses] homes of simple mind and innocence'. This proves that he was describing the ancient Badgworthy settlement, occupied for centuries by hermits and holy men. When the Doones settled in the uninhabited Royal Forest of Exmoor the only houses available to them were those that had formed this deserted medieval village. Alfred Vowles (see Reading List) traced fourteen ruined houses when he investigated the valley. We must recognise, however, that the ravages of Exmoor weather have destroyed much that was visible to him. Today, a few mounds give little idea of the ground plan that Blackmore knew and that Vowles reconstructed at the eastern extremity of Hoccombe Combe.*

*The natural features were dramatised by Blackmore. There are no mountains. The Doone Gate is imaginary. The Water Slide (see page 32) is not fearsome. A dozen different Exmoor scenes were fused to produce 'Doone Land'. Even so, the imaginative reader will always see Badgworthy through Blackmore's eyes.*

**Doone Country—and perhaps the Doone Valley**

A ND SO, in a sorry plight, I came to an opening in the bushes, where a great black pool lay in front of me . . . And the look of this black pit was enough to stop one from diving into it, even on a hot summer's day with sunshine on the water; I mean, if the sun ever shone there . . . But soon I saw the reason for the stir and depth of that great pit, as well as of the roaring sound which long had made me wonder . . . For, lo! I stood at the foot of a long pale slide of water, coming smoothly to me, without any break or hindrance, for a hundred yards or more, and fenced on either side with cliff, sheer, and straight, and shining. The water neither ran nor fell, nor leaped with any spouting, but made one even slope of it, as if it had been combed or planed, and looking like a plank of deal laid down a deep black staircase.

CHAPTER VII

*Fishing for loaches in Badgworthy Water, Jan suddenly and terrifyingly comes upon the Water Slide. With great courage (and great fear) the boy fights his way up this huge barrier and, nearly drowning, penetrates the Doone Valley, where he has his first meeting with Lorna*

*Controversy rages about the precise identification of the Water Slide. Ingenuity is strained to 'prove' that this or that combe is its original. There is little doubt that Blackmore knew Lank Combe where—on a pigmy scale compared with the description in the novel— the water does, indeed, come gliding down the rocks 'in a long pale slide'. It would be perverse to argue that Lank Combe was not the germ of the Water Slide. We must, however, keep a sense of proportion. Blackmore legitimately combined and exaggerated natural features to provide an epic background for his stirring narrative. Just as the present Lorna Doone Farm, and other old buildings round about, suggested material for Plover's Barrows, so Badgworthy, Hoccombe Combe and Lank Combe gave him the basis for his magnificent description of the Doone Valley. Blackmore does not consistently indicate that his imaginary Doone Valley was a tributary opening into Badgworthy. Had he done so, there would be some point in getting steamed up about the rival claims of Hoccombe Combe and Lank Combe.*

*As it is, let us be thankful that all this superb 'Doone Land' is readily accessible from Malmsmead: and let us use our imagination —as Blackmore used his.*

**The Water Slide?—see Inside Back Cover**

32

IT was a long flat sweep of moorland over which he was gazing, with a few bogs here and there, and brushy places round them. Of course, John Fry, from his shepherd life, and reclaiming of strayed cattle, knew as well as need be where he was, and the spread of the hills before him, although it was beyond our beat . . . but he liked it none the more for that, neither did any of our people; and, indeed, all the neighbourhood of Thomshill and Larksborough, and most of all Black Barrow Down, lay under the grave imputation of having been enchanted with a very evil spell. Moreover, it was known, though folk were loth to speak of it, even on a summer morning, that Squire Thom, who had been murdered there, a century ago or more, had been seen by several shepherds, even in the middle day, walking with his severed head carried in his left hand, and his right arm lifted towards the sun. Therefore it was very bold in John . . . to venture across that moor alone . . . For, carefully spying across the moor, from behind the tuft of whortles, at first he could discover nothing having life and motion, except three or four wild cattle roving in vain search for nourishment, and a diseased sheep banished hither, and some carrion crows keeping watch on her.

CHAPTER XXXI

*In this incident John Fry is tracking Reuben Huckaback, whose mysterious journeys into the wild moorland have excited the curiosity of the Ridds. The wily old merchant is, in fact, prospecting for the mineral wealth which he hopes to add to his already considerable store.*

*The passage is a good example of Blackmore's skill in evoking the Exmoor scene. The Doone Country (illustrated in pictures and words on pages 26—33) is surrounded by a high plateau where rolling moor lines, golden molinia grass, flying cloud shadows, lark song and curlew call exhilarate the traveller on a sunny day—in striking contrast to the eerie shapes and the stark desolation that threaten him when the mists fall or when dusk begins. Then, indeed, he quickens his steps as best he may, to be off the moor before night and its spectres overtake him.*

*The illustration shows John Knight's Forest Wall. To the north of the Wall (on its left in the photograph) is Brendon Common: south lies the Forest. Hoccombe Water sweeps down from Brendon Two Gates to its junction with Long Combe. The cleft of Badgworthy runs from right to left, while on the skyline the quagmires of Black Barrow Down and the upper reaches of Long Combe can be seen.*

**Into Doone Land—the hard way**

Now the wisest person in all our parts was reckoned to be a certain wise woman, well known all over Exmoor by the name of 'Mother Melldrum'. [She] had two . . . homes . . . according to the time of year. In summer she lived in a pleasant cave, facing the cool side of the hill, far inland near Hawkridge, and close above 'Tarr Steps', a wonderful crossing of the Barle river, made (as everybody knows) by Satan for a wager. But throughout the winter, she found sea-air agreeable, and a place where things could be had on credit, and more occasion of talking. Not but what she could have credit (for every one was afraid of her) in the neighbourhood of Tarr Steps; only there was no one handy owning things worth taking. Therefore, at the fall of the leaf, when the woods grew damp and irksome, the wise woman set her face to the warmer cliffs of the Channel; where shelter was, and dry fern bedding, and folk to be seen . . . And there . . . anyone who chose might find her, towards the close of a winter's day, gathering sticks and brown fern for fuel, and talking to herself the while, in a hollow stretch behind the cliffs; which foreigners who come and go without seeing much of Exmoor have called the 'Valley of Rocks'. This valley, or 'goyal', as we term it, lies to the west of Lynton . . . Our homefolk always call it the 'Danes', or the 'Denes'; which is no more, they tell me, than a hollow place . . . It is a green, rough-sided hollow, bending at the middle, touched with stone at either crest, and dotted here and there with slabs, in and out the brambles. On the right hand is an upward crag, called by some the 'Castle', easy enough to scale, and giving great view of the Channel. Facing this, from the inland side and the elbow of the valley, a queer old pile of rock arises, bold behind one another, and quite enough to affright a man . . . This is called the 'Devil's Cheese-ring' or the 'Devil's Cheese-knife', which means the same thing, as our fathers were used to eat their cheese from a scoop; and perhaps in old time the upmost rock . . . was like to such an implement if Satan eat cheese untoasted . . . Now Mother Melldrum kept her winter in this vale of rocks, sheltering from the wind and rain within the Devil's Cheese-ring; which added greatly to her fame, because all else, for miles around, were afraid to go near it after dark, or even on a gloomy day.

CHAPTER XVII

*John Ridd, however, has the courage to consult Mother Melldrum about his love for Lorna Doone. His interview with the wise woman is terminated by defiance on his part and oracular words from her. Then comes the famous fight between the 'fine fat sheep' and the 'lean black goat'. The Valley of Rocks is a dry valley, once the course of the two Lyn Rivers, and now weathered and eroded into fantastic shapes. (Black-more's spelling 'Cheese-ring' conforms to the belief that the rock resem-bles a 'scoop' or 'ring'. The latter-day spelling, 'Wring', suggests a likeness to a 'press').*

**'The Devil's Cheese-wring'.**

WHILE John was trembling within himself . . . to his great amazement something white arose out of the hole, under the brown trunk of the tree. Seeing this his blood went back within him; yet he was not able to turn and flee, but rooted his face in among the loose stones, and kept his quivering shoulders back, and prayed to God to protect him. However, the white thing itself was not so very awful, being nothing more than a long-coned night-cap with a tassel on the top, such as criminals wear at hanging-time. But when John saw a man's face under it, and a man's neck and shoulders slowly rising out of the pit, he could not doubt that this was the place where the murderers come to life again, according to the Exmoor story. He knew that a man had been hanged last week, and that this was the ninth day after it.

Therefore he could bear no more . . . neither did he wait to see what became of the gallows-man; but climbed on his horse with what speed he might, and rode away at full gallop. Neither did he dare go back the way he came, fearing to face Black Barrow Down. Therefore he struck up the other track leading away towards Cloven Rocks, and after riding hard for an hour and drinking all his whiskey, he luckily fell in with a shepherd, who led him on to a public-house somewhere near Exford. And here he was so unmanned, the excitement being over, that nothing less than a gallon of ale and half a gammon of bacon, brought him to his right mind again. And he took good care to be home before dark, having followed a well-known sheep-track.

CHAPTER XXXI

*John Fry's stalking of Reuben Huckaback (see page 34) culminates in this alarming incident. In fact, John has unwittingly stumbled on the secret of Reuben's mine which, as we have seen, (page 22) plays an important part in the plot. The blend of tension, humour, local legend and vivid description is typical of Blackmore at his best.*

*Topographically, the material is of great interest: ' a public house somewhere near Exford' (where John Fry consumes such modest quantities of beer and bacon!) may be confidently identified as Red Deer—once known as Gallon House. However, the wording "somewhere near Exford" should put us on our guard against dogmatic pin-pointings: Red Deer is almost exactly half-way between Exford and Simonsbath. Cloven Rocks and Black Barrow are real places and Blackmore sites them accurately. Yet he leaves romantically and conveniently vague the precise spatial relationship between those two key-points, Plover's Barrows and the Wizard's Slough. We shall have to return to this topic later.*

**Red Deer or Gallon House**

IT appears that as he [Jeremy Stickles] was riding towards us, from the town of South Molton in Devonshire, he found the roads very soft and heavy, and the floods out in all directions; but met with no other danger until he came to Landacre Bridge. He had only a single trooper with him, a man . . . whom Jeremy had brought from Exeter. As these two descended towards the bridge, they observed that both the Kensford Water and the River Barle were pouring down in mighty floods . . . only the parapets of the bridge could be seen above the water . . . On the crown of the bridge [Jeremy] turned his horse to watch the trooper's passage, and to help him with directions; when suddenly he saw him fall headlong into the torrent, and heard the report of a gun from behind, and felt a shock to his own body, such as lifted him out of the saddle. Turning round he beheld three men, risen up from behind the hedge on one side of his onward road . . . he struck the spurs into the nag and rode through the water straight at the man who was pointing the long gun at him . . . 'If they do not catch me up, or shoot me, in the course of the first two miles, I may see my home again,' this was what he said to himself, as he turned to mark what they were about, from the brow of the steep hill. He saw the flooded valley shining with the breadth of water, and the trooper's horse on the other side . . . and half-way down the hill he saw the three Doones mounting hastily. And then he knew that his only chance lay in the stoutness of his steed.

CHAPTER XLVII

*Jeremy Stickles, King's Messenger, plays an important part in the novel.  His job is to investigate the anti-papist movements that led so many men from the Exmoor area to the fatal field of Sedgemoor and to the Bloody Assizes.  He also keeps a sharp eye on the Doones; and the Doones are out to get him.*

*The whole of Chapter XLVII repays most careful reading and I regret that space does not permit extended quotation.  However, if 'The Lorna Doone Trail' sends its readers back to Blackmore, it will have done its work.*

*Gripping as a narrative, the chapter throws light on Blackmore's handling of place and scene.  Precision of location and deliberate vagueness are both employed. (Kensford Water, by the way, is 'Kinsford', the upper course of Sherdon.)  Landacre Bridge is a well-known and beautiful Exmoor feature.  The old Swainmote Court used to be held there.  'Landacre—Withycombe—Newland— the Exe': spot on!  Jeremy's route can be plotted.  'Passed towards Lucott Hill—struck upon the founts of Lyn—arrived at Plover's Barrows': general direction clear enough, but all detail omitted.*

**Landacre Bridge**

For he loved a maid of South Molton (a currier's daughter I think she was, and her name was Betsy Paramore), and her father had given consent; and Tom Faggus, wishing to look his best, and be clean of course, had a tailor at work upstairs for him, who had come all the way from Exeter. And Betsy's things were ready too—for which they accused him afterwards, as if he could help that—when suddenly . . . a lawyer's writ fell upon him . . . Sir Robert could pay for much swearing; and then all his goods and his farm were sold up, and even his smithery taken. But he saddled his horse, before they could catch him, and rode away to South Molton, looking more like a madman than a good farrier, as the people said who saw him. But when he arrived there, instead of comfort, they showed him the face of the door alone; for the news of his loss was before him, and Master Paramore was a sound prudent man, and a high member of the town-council. It is said that they even gave him notice to pay for Betsy's wedding-clothes, now that he was too poor to marry her. This may be false, and indeed I doubt it; in the first place, because South Molton is a busy place for talking; and in the next, that I do not think the action would have lain at law, especially as the maid lost nothing, but used it all for her wedding next month with Dick Vellacott.

CHAPTER XII

'And how was it you were struck by a bullet, and only shaken in your saddle? Had you a coat of mail on, or of Milanese chain-armour? Now, Master Stickles, had you?'

'No, Mistress Lizzie; we do not wear things of that kind nowadays. You are apt, I perceive, at romances. But I happened to have a little flat bottle of the best stoneware slung beneath my saddle-cloak, and filled with the very best *eau de vie* from the George Hotel, at South Molton. The brand of it now is upon my back. Oh, the murderous scoundrels, what a brave spirit they have spilled!'

CHAPTER XLVII


*So often, the 'yellow' roads on our maps were the chief routes of times past—times when many of our present trunk and main roads did not exist. The South Molton—North Molton—Sandyway—Withypool—Winsford route was an Exmoor lifeline: a reason for the part that this delightful Devonshire town plays in the novel. No reader of 'Lorna Doone' can leave South Molton unvisited. Local Government reorganisation may have dimmed its civic dignity, but the George—praise be!—flourishes. The Guildhall is lovely yet. The Market House, Medical Hall, St. Mary Magdalene and the Town Museum offer hours of interest. 'A busy place for talking', says John Ridd—certainly a place to be talked about.*

**The Guildhall, South Molton**

In very quick time, I ran away with the shilling in my pocket, and got Peggy out on the Porlock road, without my mother knowing it. For mother was frightened of that road now, as if all the trees were murderers . . . And, to tell the truth, I was touched with fear for many years about it; and even now, when I ride at dark there, a man by a peat rick makes me shiver until I go and collar him. But this time I was very bold, having John Fry's blunderbuss, and keeping a sharp look-out wherever any lurking-place was. However, I saw only sheep, and small red cattle, and the common deer of the forest, until I was near to Porlock town, and then rode straight to Mr. Pooke's, at the sign of the Spit and Gridiron.

Mr. Pooke was asleep, as it happened, not having much to do that day . . . and in I walked with a manful style, bearing John Fry's blunderbuss. Now Timothy Pooke was a peaceful man, glad to live without any enjoyment of mind at danger, and I was tall and large already, as most lads of a riper age. Mr. Pooke, as soon as he opened his eyes, dropped suddenly under the counter-board and drew a great frying-pan over his head, as if the Doones were come to rob him . . .

'Gadzooks, Master Pooke,' said I, having learned fine words at Tiverton, 'do you suppose that I know not then the way to carry firearms?'

. . . 'God sake, John Ridd, God sake, dear boy,' cried Pooke, knowing me by this time: 'don't 'ee, for good love now, don't 'ee show it to me, boy, as if I were to suck it. Put 'un down, for good, now; and thee shall have the very best of all is in the shop.'

But in spite of all assurances, he showed himself desirous only to see the last of my gun and me . . . For my shilling Master Pooke afforded me two great packages [of gunpowder] . . . as well as a mighty chunk of lead . . . And as if all this had not been enough, he presented me with a roll of comfits for my sister Annie, whose gentle face and pretty manners won the love of everybody.

CHAPTER VI

*John's journey takes him along the fatal road on which his father was murdered when returning from Porlock market (see Chapter IV). Practice with his father's long gun fits him for the battle with the Doones that must come.*

*Porlock was a busy town, catering for the needs of North Exmoor folk. Surrounded by truly fertile land and linked with Porlock Weir— through which so many goods were imported (some paid Excise Duty; many did not)—it was conscious of its own importance. The Ship Inn, at the foot of Porlock Hill, was the scene of one of Tom Faggus's exploits.*

**The Ship Inn, Porlock**

B Y dinner-time we [Jeremy Stickles and John Ridd] arrived at Porlock, and dined with my old friend, Master Pooke, now growing rich and portly. For though we had plenty of victuals with us, we were not to begin upon them, until all chance of victualling among our friends was left behind. And during that first day we had no need to meddle with our store at all; for as had been settled before we left home, we lay that night at Dunster, in the house of a worthy tanner, first cousin to my mother, who received us very cordially, and undertook to return old Smiler to his stable at Plover's Barrows, after one day's rest. Thence we hired to Bridgwater; and from Bridgwater on to Bristowe [Bristol], breaking the journey between the two . . . And when I let it be known, by some hap, that I was the own cousin of Tom Faggus, and honoured with his society, there was not a house on the road but was proud to entertain me, in spite of my fellow-traveller bearing the red badge of the King.

'I will keep this close, my son Jack,' he said, having stripped it off with a carving-knife; 'your flag is the best to fly.'

Therefore we pursued our way, in excellent condition, having thriven upon the credit of that very popular highwayman, and being surrounded with regrets that he had left the profession . . .

It was a long and weary journey, although the roads are wondrous good on the further side of Bristowe, and scarcely any man need be bogged, if he keeps his eyes well open, save, perhaps, in Berkshire.

CHAPTER XXIV

*Escorted by Jeremy Stickles, John Ridd is on his way to London to 'appear in person before the Right Worshipful the Justices of His Majesty's Bench at Westminster . . . there to deliver such evidence as is within thy cognizance, touching certain matters whereby the peace of our said lord the King . . . is . . . impeached, impugned, imperilled, or otherwise detrimented' (see Chapter XXIII). The passage throws an interesting light on the discomforts and perils of 17th century travel and, of course, builds up the fame of Tom Faggus. It also accurately outlines the West Country route to London.*

*We cannot know which Dunster house Blackmore envisaged as the home of Mrs. Ridd's cousin. That in the foreground of the illustration would be a possibility, but Dunster abounds in old and beautiful buildings.*

**Dunster: such a house as John Ridd might have known**

46

IT was the beginning of wheat-harvest, when I came to Dunster town, having walked all the way from London, and being somewhat footsore. For though five pounds was enough to keep me in food and lodging upon the road, it would have been nothing for horse-hire, as I knew too well by the prices Jeremy Stickles had paid, upon our way to London. Now I never saw a prettier town than Dunster looked that evening; for sooth to say, I had almost lost all hope of reaching it that night, although the castle was long in view. But being once there my troubles were gone, at least as regarded way-faring; for mother's cousin . . .was in such indignation at the plight in which I came to him, afoot, and weary, and almost shoeless . . . that he swore then, by the mercy of God, that if the schemes abrew-ing round him, against those bloody Papists, should come to any shape, and show good chance of succeeding, he would risk a thou-sand pounds, as though it were a penny . . . I think I made him know that the bad state in which I came to his town, and the great shame I had wrought for him among the folk round the card-table at the Luttrell Arms was not to be, even there, attributed to King Charles the Second, nor even to his counsellors, but to my own speed of travelling, which had beat post-horses. For being much distraught in mind, and desperate in body, I had made all the way from London to Dunster in six days, and no more. It may be one hundred and seventy miles, I cannot tell to a furlong or two, especially as I had lost my way more than a dozen times; but at any rate there in six days I was, and most kindly they received me.

CHAPTER XXVII

*During his first visit to London John Ridd suffers much from 'the law's delay'. He is not called before the Justices and he receives no payment towards his living expenses. A smooth rogue of a lawyer called Spanks pockets John's allowance and attempts to extort fees from him. John's transparent honesty and outspokenness bring him favourable treatment from Judge Jeffreys when, at last, a lucky chance puts him in that terrifying man's way. Spank is discomfited and offers John reparation. His contempt for the upright yeoman knows no bounds when he refuses to take a penny more than his out-of-pocket expenses. (Hence the mere five pounds with which John set out on the long journey home.)*

*The illustration shows a corner of the famous Yarn Market and the noble porch of the Luttrell Arms.*

**Architectural perfection at Dunster**

Now, all the towns of Somersetshire and half the towns of Devonshire were full of pushing eager people, ready to swallow anything . . . Taunton, Bridgwater, Minehead and Dulverton took the lead of the other towns in utterance of their discontent, and threats of what they meant to do, if ever a Papist dared to climb the Protestant throne of England. So the Tory policy was to watch . . . and then to strike severely. And as a Tory watchman—or spy, as the Whigs would call him—Jeremy Stickles was now among us: and his duty was threefold. First . . . to see to the levying of poundage in the little haven of Lynmouth, and further up the coast . . . Second, his duty was to watch [the Doones] narrowly . . . Jeremy Stickles' third business was entirely political; to learn the temper of our people and the gentle families . . . to discover any collecting of arms and drilling of men . . . to prevent . . . any importation of gunpowder . . . in a word to observe and forestall the enemy.

CHAPTER XXXIX

[Jeremy] agreed with me that we could not hope to escape an attack from the outlaws, and the more especially now that they knew himself to be returned to us . . . and he thought it wiser that I should go . . . to Lynmouth, if a horse could pass the valley, and fetch every one of his mounted troopers . . . Knowing how fiercely the floods were out, I resolved to travel the higher road, by Cosgate and through Countisbury; therefore I swam my horse through the Lyn . . . and thence galloped up and along the hills. I could see all the inland valleys ribboned with broad waters . . . but when I descended the hill towards Lynmouth, I feared that my journey was all in vain. For the East Lyn . . . was ramping and roaring frightfully, lashing whole trunks of trees on the rocks, and rending them, and grinding them . . . It was certain death to attempt the passage; and the little wooden footbridge had been carried away long ago.

CHAPTER XLVIII

*In the extract from Chapter XXXIX Blackmore's skill in setting the Ridd-Doone story against a credible and historically-based background is evident. Only a careful reading of the book can do him justice, though. In Chapter XLVIII John makes a perilous journey to fetch help. Follow this extract on the Ordnance Map. His usual route would have been through Slocombeslade, Tippacott and the valley road to Lynmouth. His description of the raging Lyn reminds us of 15-16 August 1952. 'Cosgate' is County Gate. At Countisbury a fine church and inn introduce the precipitous descent into Lynmouth. Near the hamlet is the site of Arx Cynuit where, in 878, Ealdorman Odda's men routed a Danish army.*

**The Blue Ball, Countisbury**

B ut during those two months of fog (for we had it all the winter) the saddest and the heaviest thing was to stand by the sea. To be upon the beach yourself, and see the long waves coming in; to know that they are long waves, but only see a piece of them; and to hear them lifting roundly, swelling over smooth green rocks, lashing down in the hollow corners, but bearing on all the same as ever, soft and sleek and sorrowful, till their little noise is over.

One old man who lived at Lynmouth, seeking to be buried there, having been more than half over the world . . . this old Will Watcombe (who dwelt by the water) said that our strange winter arose from a thing he called the 'Gulf-stream' rushing up channel suddenly. He said it was hot water, almost fit for a man to shave with, and it threw all our cold water out, and ruined the fish and spawning-time, and a cold spring would come after it. I was fond of going to Lynmouth on Sunday to hear this old man talk . . . He told me that this powerful flood set in upon our coast so hard, sometimes once in ten years, and sometimes not for fifty . . . but that when it came, therewith came warmth, and clouds, and fog, and moisture, and nuts, and fruit, and even shells . . . As for nuts he winked awhile, and chewed a piece of tobacco . . . Afterwards I heard that nuts with liquid kernels came, travelling on the Gulf-stream; for never before was so much foreign cordial landed upon our coast, floating ashore by mistake in the fog . . . too much astray to learn its duty . . . Folk said that Will Watcombe himself knew better than anybody else about this drift of the Gulf-stream, and the places where it would come ashore, and the cave that took the indraught . . . We common people joked of the 'Gulp-stream', as we called it.

But the thing which astonished and frightened us . . . was a strange mysterious sound . . . It mattered not whether you stood on the moor, or crouched behind rocks away from it . . . there was rushing of something by and melancholy laughter, and the hair of a man would stand on end . . . Those who heard it most often declared that it must be the wail of a woman's voice, and the rustle of robes fleeing horribly, and fiends in the fog going after her.

CHAPTER XII

*Of all the western moors, only Exmoor has a coast. The sea, shipping and smuggling have always played a large part in its story. Though the little ports—Lynmouth, Porlock Weir, Minehead and Watchet—are not 'central' to the novel, Blackmore makes us conscious of their presence and their influence. This passage is a good example of his skilful blending of sea and moor when creating atmosphere.*

**Quay Street: near the Harbour, Minehead**

H ow far call you it now to the bank of the sea at Wash—Wash-?'
'At Watchet, likely you mean, madam. Oh, a very long way,
and the roads as soft as the road to Oare.'

CHAPTER III

Therefore . . . the horses were put to again, and the heavy coach
went up the hill, with the lady and her two children, and Benita,
sitting inside of it . . . Much had been said at Dulverton, and even
back at Bampton, about some great freebooters, to whom all Exmoor owed suit and service . . . Through the fog, and through the
muck, the coach went on . . . to the pitch and the slope of the sea-
bank, leading on towards Watchet town . . . and there they met their
fate, and could not fly it . . . The silver light showed them a troop
of horsemen . . . ready to dash upon them . . . Meanwhile the drivers
drove into the sea . . . but before the waves came into the coach,
a score of fierce men were around it . . . What followed, Benita
knew not . . . being stunned by a blow on the head, beside being
palsied with terror . . . But when she recovered her senses, she found
herself upon the sand; the robbers were out of sight . . . Then she
arose and ran to her mistress, who was sitting upright on a little
rock, with her dead boy's face to her bosom, sometimes gazing
upon him, and sometimes questioning round for the other one.

CHAPTER LIII

*And so, the John Ridd-Lorna Doone story, so fortuitously begun at
an inn at Dulverton, begins to untangle its ravelled skein. Jeremy
Stickles tells John of his encounter with Benita, concluding trium-
phantly: 'That little maid [the child abducted from the coach by the
Doones] is Lorna Doone.'*

*John's own later visit to Watchet results in a meeting between
Lorna and Benita. Their recognition of each other and the network
of circumstantial evidence, carefully woven by Blackmore, establishes
Lorna's identity as Lady Lorna Dugal, daughter of 'a nobleman of high
and goodly lineage' and of a mother 'of yet more ancient and renowned
descent' (Chapter LVIII). In abducting Lorna the Doones hoped
to secure her property by forcing her to marry Carver and, at
the same time, to exact an exquisite revenge on the Earl of Lorne,
whose daughter had been unwise enough to marry Sir Ensor Doone.*

**Watchet Harbour**

BEFORE the light of morning came along the tide to Watchet my Lady met her husband. They took her into the town that night, but not to her own castle; and so the power of womanhood (which is itself maternity) came over-swiftly upon her. The lady . . . lies in Watchet little churchyard, with son and heir at her right hand, and a little babe . . . sleeping on her bosom.

CHAPTER LIII

When I heard that Lorna's father was the Earl of Dugal . . . I never thought but everybody in Watchet town must know all about the tombstone of the Countess of Dugal. This however proved otherwise. For Lord Dugal had never lived at Watchet Grange, as their place was called, neither had his name become familiar as its owner . . . And upon news of his death, John Jones, a rich gentleman from Llandaff, had taken possession, as next of right, and hushed up all the story . . . So the poor Countess of Dugal, almost in sight of her own grand house, was buried in an unknown grave, together with her pair of infants, without a plate, without a tombstone (worse than all), without a tear, except from the hired Italian woman. Surely my poor Lorna came of an ill-starred family . . . All Watchet town cared ten times as much to see John Ridd, as to show him what he wanted. I was led to every public-house instead of the churchyard; and twenty tables were ready for me, in lieu of a single grave-stone. 'Zummersett thou bee'st, Jan Ridd, and Zummerzett thou shalt be . . . Whoy, thee lives in Zummerzett; and in Zummerzett thee wast barn, lad.' And so it went on, till I was weary; though very much obliged to them.

CHAPTER LVI

Having obtained from Benita . . . a very close and full description of the place where her poor mistress lay, and the marks whereby to know it, I hastened to Watchet the following morning, before the sun was up, or any people were about . . . In the furthest and darkest nook, overgrown with grass, and overhung by a weeping tree, a little bank of earth betokened the rounding off of a hapless life. There was nothing to tell of rank, or wealth, or love, or even pity . . . I gathered a little grass for Lorna, and a sprig of the weeping tree.

CHAPTER LVII

*Lorna's mother was journeying to Watchet, not to take ship there but to wait at the Grange for her husband's return from abroad. She did not live long enough to know that he was dead.*

*The hill-top church attracts many visitors—its site may have inspired Coleridge—but a search for the grave of Lorna's mother will hardly be fruitful!*

**St. Decuman's, Watchet**

L ORNA'S dress was of pure white, clouded with faint lavender . . . and as simple as need be, except for perfect loveliness. I was afraid to look at her . . . except when each of us said, 'I will', and then each dwelled upon the other. It is impossible for any, who have not loved as I have, to conceive my joy and pride, when after ring and all was done, and the parson had blessed us, Lorna turned to look at me, with her playful glance subdued, and deepened by this solemn act.

Her eyes, which none on earth may ever equal, or compare with, told me such a tale of hope and faith, and heart's devotion, that I was almost amazed, thoroughly as I knew them. Darling eyes, the clearest eyes, the loveliest, the most loving eyes—the sound of a shot rang through the church, and those eyes were dim with death.

Lorna fell across my knees, when I was going to kiss her, as the bridegroom is allowed to do, and encouraged, if he needs it; a flood of blood came out upon the yellow wood of the altar steps; and at my feet lay Lorna, trying to tell me some last message out of her faithful eyes. I lifted her up, and petted her, and coaxed her, but it was no good; the only sign of life remaining was a drip of bright red blood.

Some men know what things befall them in the supreme time of their life—far above the time of death—but to me comes back as a hazy dream, without any knowledge of it, what I did, or felt, or thought, with my wife's arms flagging round my neck, as I raised her up, and softly put them there. She sighed a long sigh on my breast, for her last farewell to life, and then she grew so cold, and cold, that I asked the time of year.

It was now Whit-Tuesday, and the lilacs all in blossom; and why I thought of the time of year, with the young death in my arms, God or His angels may decide . . . Enough that I did, and looked; and our white lilacs were beautiful. Then I laid my wife in my mother's arms, and begging that no one would make a noise, went forth for my revenge.

CHAPTER LXXIV

*From the sacking of the Doone Valley and the trap set for the out-laws at the Warren, of the able-bodied only Carver escaped. 'It was,' as John says (Chapter LXII) 'no light thing to have a man of such power, and resource, and desperation, left at large and furious, like a famished wolf round the sheep-fold.' And now the wolf has preyed. When John goes forth to his revenge, unarmed, he is convinced that Lorna is dead.*

*A notice in Oare church draws attention to 'the Carver window': a copy of the famous medallion portrait in Exeter Cathedral does honour to Blackmore.*

**St. Mary's, Oare**

I CAME upon Barrow Down . . . and there, about a furlong before me, rode a man on a great black horse; and I knew that the man was Carver Doone . . . He turned up the gully leading from the moor to Cloven Rocks, through which John Fry had tracked Uncle Ben, as of old related. But as Carver entered it, he turned round, and beheld me not a hundred yards behind; and I saw that he was bearing his child, little Ensie, before him. Ensie also descried me, and stretched his hands, and cried to me; for the face of his father frightened him . . .

Carver drew rein at the crossways sharply, and plunged into the black ravine leading to the Wizard's Slough . . . Now there is a way between cliff and slough, for those who know the ground thoroughly; but for him there was no road . . . Upon this he made up his mind; and wheeling, fired and then rode at me. His bullet struck me somewhere, but I took no heed of that. Fearing only his escape, I laid my horse across the way . . . Ere the slash of the sword came nigh me, man and horse rolled over . . . With a sullen and black scowl, the Carver gathered his mighty limbs . . . I think that he felt his time was come. I think he knew from my knitted muscles, and the firm arch of my breast; but most of all from my stern blue eyes, that he had met his master.

Carver Doone caught me round the waist, with such a grip as never yet had been laid upon me. I heard my rib go . . . then I took him by the throat. In vain he tugged, and strained, and writhed, dashed his bleeding fist into my face. I had him helpless in two minutes, and his blazing eyes lolled out . . . The black bog had him by the feet; the sucking of the ground drew on him, like the thirsty lips of death. In our fury, we had heeded neither wet nor dry, nor thought of the earth beneath us . . . He fell back . . . like a hummock of bog-oak, standing out of the quagmire; and then he tossed his arms to heaven, and they were black to the elbow, and the glare of his eyes was ghastly. I could only gaze and pant: for my strength was no more than an infant's, from the fury and the horror. Scarcely could I turn away, while, joint by joint, he sank from sight.

CHAPTER LXXIV


*This famous passage has set many a reader searching for the Wizard's Slough. Blackmore gives some clues, but omits the vital ones. The chase over Black Barrow Down can be followed, but the 'crossways' and 'the black ravine' cannot be identified. Again, the killing power of this bog is not matched by any Exmoor quagmire. Cloven Rocks, if it ever tallied with this description, must have changed quite a lot, but the romantics among us may well like to think of it as the site of the dreaded Wizard's Slough*

**Near Cloven Rocks**

A s for Lorna . . . she never tires of being with me here and there, among the beautiful places, and talking with her arm around me—so far at least as it can go—of the many fears, and troubles, dangers and discouragements, and worst of all the bitter partings, which we used to undergo.

There is no need for my farming harder than becomes a man of weight. Lorna has great stores of money, though we never draw it out, except for some poor neighbour; unless I find her a sumptuous dress, out of her own perquisites. And this she always looks upon as a wondrous gift from me; and kisses me much when she puts it on, and walks like the noble woman she is. And yet I may never behold it again; for she gets back to her simple clothes and I love her the better in them. I believe that she gives half the grandeur away, and keeps the other half for the children . . .

Jeremy Stickles was glad to help Tom Faggus in getting a pardon . . . Thereafter, the good and respectable Tom lived a godly and righteous (though not always sober) life; and brought up his children to honesty, as the first of all qualifications.

My dear mother was as happy as possibly need be with us; having no cause for jealousy, as others arose around her . . . I sent little Ensie to Blundell's School, at my own cost and charges, having changed his name, for fear of what anyone might do to him. I called him 'Ensie Jones' and I hope that he will be a credit to us . . .

Of Lorna, of my lifelong darling, of my more and more loved wife, I will not talk; for it is not seemly, that a man should exalt his pride. Year by year, her beauty grows, with the growth of goodness, kindness, and true happiness—above all with loving. For change, she makes a joke of this, and plays with it, and laughs at it; and then, when my slow nature marvels, back she comes to the earnest thing. And if I wish to pay her out for something very dreadful—as may happen once or twice, when we become too gladsome—I bring her to forgotten sadness, and to me for cure of it, by the two words, 'Lorna Doone'.

CHAPTER LXXV

*Yes, it is a fairy-tale ending—but that, surely, is how a romance should end. Cured by Ruth's skill in medicine, Lorna is restored to John; and they live happily ever after.*

*Let us imagine them, as Blackmore wished us to, living their peaceful lives in the parish of Oare, in the County of Somerset: Sir John Ridd, yeoman and churchwarden and his noble wife.*

**The porch at Oare**

# Reading List

Blackmore, R. D.: *Lorna Doone*. Various publishers, 1st ed. 1869.

Blackmore R. D.: *Springhaven*. Dent (Everyman's Library, No. 350), 1st ed. 1887.

Browne, Ida M. (Audrie Doon): *A Short History of the Original Doones of Exmoor*. Cox, Williton, 1901.

Budd, K.: *The Last Victorian*. Centaur Press, 1960.

Burton, S. H.: *Exmoor*. Robert Hale, 4th ed. 1984.

Cooper, Cicely E.: *R. D. Blackmore's Other Books*. Exmoor Review, 1973.

Dunn, W. H.: *R. D. Blackmore*. Robert Hale, 1955.

Eardley Wilmot, H.: *Yesterday's Exmoor*. Exmoor Books, 1990.

Oakeley, A.: *Lorna Doone: The Facts*. Published by the author.

Rawle, E. J.: *The Doones of Exmoor*. Barnicott, Taunton, 1903.

Vowles, A.: *The Doone Valley and Water-Slide of 'Lorna Doone'*. Cox, Williton, 1929.

## Microstudies

All the titles in this series, published by The Exmoor Press, Dulverton, should be read by those interested in Exmoor. Of particular relevance are:

Allen, N. V.: *Churches and Chapels of Exmoor*, 1974.

Allen, N. V.: *The Waters of Exmoor*, 1978.

Eardley-Wilmot, Hazel: *Ancient Exmoor*, 1983.

Farr, Grahame: *Ships and Harbours of Exmoor*, 1970.

Hurley, Jack: *Legends of Exmoor*, 1973.

Hurley, Jack: *Murder and Mystery on Exmoor*, 4th ed., 1982.

Lawrence, Berta: *Exmoor Villages*, 1984.

Patten, R. W.: *Exmoor Custom and Song*, 1974.